Appetizers from the Word of God

Are you Hungry?

SALVATION PEACE HEALING JOY

Volume Two

Black & White Printed Edition

Minister Linda C. Mason

Appetizers from the Word of God...Are You Hungry?

Volume 2, Black & White Printed Edition

Newly Revised Edition

By: Minister Linda C. Mason

Published by:
Deep Sea Publishing, LLC
1109 Devon Street
Herndon, VA 20170
sales@deepseapublishing.com

Color Print:
ISBN-13: 978-1-939535-26-9
ISBN-10: 1939535263
B/W Print:
ISBN-13: 978-1-939535-28-3
ISBN-10: 193953528X
E-Book:
ISBN-13: 978-1-939535-27-6
ISBN-10: 1939535271

Cover Design by Matthew Williams, Sr.

All scriptural quotations are taken from the King James Version of the Bible (KJV) unless otherwise noted.

Printed in the United States of America.

INTRODUCTION

Once we begin to study the Word of God, we come to know that it will take us a lifetime to comprehend as much as God desires us to, because our desires will always increase for more of Him as we continue to study. I believe the Lord designed it that way. Because God is a spirit, we were designed by Him with spiritual ears, spiritual eyes, a spiritual mind, and a spiritual heart that can tune in to Him--***if*** our spiritual radars have been aligned to God's channels of communication. We must tune our channel frequency to ***JESUS CHRIST***. We can find out about Him in His Word-- The Bible.

We were all designed by God to worship Him. But He gives us complete control over our own will, as we make our choices in life. Will those choices include Him, or not include Him? He tells us in Deuteronomy to choose life, but He still leaves that option up to us.

In reading this book before you, I challenge you to go beyond what is written on the pages in order to benefit from the things you will be exposed to. **This book, or any other book should never take the place of the Bible in your life;** however, I do believe that God has anointed individuals with gifts to help others understand what He wants to reveal to them in His Word. My goal is to give you easy access to what God has to say about various topics from His Word. It is still your responsibility to ***"study the Word to show thyself approved."*** Never take what anyone writes as the final authority about the Word of God. Compare what is said in books with what God says in His Word. Even if you find it in the Bible, you must learn to depend on the Holy Spirit (your true teacher) to confirm truth to you. Remember, that the "***letter of the Word"*** can kill you, but the "***spirit of the Word"*** brings life. My desire is for you to receive life.

In the collection of materials in this Volume, as well as those to follow, you will be given information and scriptural references about each topic that will help you believe God for your victories. However, you will also only be given enough so that you will become thirsty for more, and be motivated to go after more of Him. The Word of God is not as complicated as you may think. Look at the material in these volumes. You can see that this is not complicated at all. The Bible says that ***in all thy getting, get understanding.*** It is the understanding that will produce wisdom in your choices. Wisdom is the ***wise application*** of the information and knowledge that you obtain. Without wise application, you will only produce frustration and stagnation in your life.

Volume One takes you through the salvation series. If you are not sure you are saved, I suggest strongly that you start with Volume One. You will then be better prepared to handle the meatier things of God found in Volumes Two and Three. If that is not possible at this time, a prayer to help you is found in the Appendix of this Volume. You may turn there now if you'd like.

These are just **"mini teachings, within a three volume series;"** (appetizers to awaken your taste buds of the spirit for more of Jesus), and by no means will cover everything God wants to let you know concerning each topic. This book may also be used as a study guide. As you venture out into the deep with these writings (expressed with simplicity), allow God's Holy Spirit to be your real teacher, and may you truly come to understand the breath, length, height, and depth of God's amazing love for you. It is my desire that you produce ***good fruit*** that remains, so that God will say to you, ***"Well done, my good and faithful servant."***

ACKNOWLEDGEMENTS & SPECIAL THANKS

You alone, O Lord, deserve all the honor and the glory! You are indeed the engine that drives me to be all You created me to be. I thank You for Your soft voice in the wee hours of the morning that never fails to guide me into Your truths. I even thank You for Your gentle rebukes of correction when I stray or just want to have my own way. You are the joy in my life, and the driving force that led me to complete the first two of three volumes in the series I hold before You now. You are such a keeper of promises. Thank You.

To the intercessory team of Emmanuel Restoration Church, thank you as well; Minister Melanie Little, Ann Walker, Hope Greene, and Pastor Nona Mason. What a foundation you have helped me lay, as I continue to move from glory to glory in the things God has called me to do.

I thank Mable Mason. You are my dearest mother-in-law and I know you are also one of my silent personal intercessors, as well. Even through all the challenges you face day to day in your own life, I know you keep me and my family lifted in prayer. Without prayer, none of this would have even gotten off the ground.

To my husband, George B. Mason, Jr. who continues to understand and respect the special calling God has on my life, I thank you. For all the hidden things you do for me, and for all the things you reveal to me---I thank you for your heart.

To my darling daughter, Tamara Mason: I thank you for helping me with the title for this book, editing this and other volumes, as well as for numerous other goodies along the way. Your wisdom continues to amaze me.

To Pastor Nona Mason of Emmanuel Restoration Church: How honored I am to have had you to step in, without much notice, and assist in the final proofing process of my book. You are a jewel in God's sight and in mine, as well. May your heavenly and earthly account multiply, as these volumes reach the multitudes for God's Glory.

Table of Contents

We all start with the same thing on our plates---NOTHING!

Appetizer 1

HOLY SPIRIT...WHAT'S THAT?

The Holy Spirit is actually the third person of the Godhead. This person is not an "it," but a person. When we receive Jesus as our Lord and Savior, the Holy Spirit is involved. He actually places or baptizes us into Jesus Christ. Once we are saved, and later receive the baptism with the Holy Spirit, Jesus Christ is the person who does that baptizing. **It is two different experiences and serves different functions in our lives.**

It is almost like being ***submerged*** into water verses ***drinking water***. There is a big difference between having water on the ***outside*** of us, and having water ***inside*** of us; yet, we need both. The water on the outside of us will keep us fresh and clean (pleasant for the eyes and to the nose), which is needed. This is an example of the Holy Spirit we receive when we are born again.

The water on the inside of us will keep us alive and healthy. This is an example of receiving the baptism with the Holy Spirit, once we have already been saved.

"And it came to pass, that while Apollos was at Corinth, Paul having passed through the upper coasts came to Ephesus: and finding certain disciples, He said unto them, Have ye received the Holy Ghost since ye believed?"

The Holy Spirit dwells in us to empower us for the work of the ministry.

- ***He sanctifies:*** ***"God hath from the beginning chosen you to salvation through sanctification of the Spirit and belief of the truth." -2 Thessalonians 2:13***

- ***He strengthens our inner man: "I pray that out of His glorious riches He may strengthen you with power through his Spirit in your inner being, so that Christ may dwell in your hearts through faith." -Ephesians 3:16***

- ***He transforms us into the character of God: "With unveiled face, beholding as in a mirror the glory of the Lord, are being transformed in the same image from glory to glory, just as by the Spirit of the Lord." -2 Corinthians 3:18***

- ***He builds by praying through us: "Building yourselves up in the most holy faith, praying in the Holy Spirit." -Jude 1:20***

- ***He gives us power: "Be strengthened with might through His Spirit." -Ephesians 3:16***

Notes as I Study the Word of God

What is the main subject of this book of the Bible?

____

Bible Verses of Focus

____
____
____
____

Chapter Outline:

____
____
____
____
____
____
____
____
____
____
____
____
____
____

What I've learned through this study of God's Word

How will I apply what I've learned to my life

Did I remember to pray today? ________

Date ______________

Appetizer 2

NAMES OF THE HOLY SPIRIT

Names, as we well know, are important. In scripture all names have special and unique meanings. This is also true of the Holy Spirit's names because we know that the Holy Spirit is a person, not an "**it**".

Below is a list of a few names of the Holy Spirit that have been revealed to us through scripture.

- **The Spirit of God**
- **The Spirit of the Lord Jehovah**
- **The Spirit of the Living God**
- **The Spirit of His Son**
- **The Spirit of Jesus Christ**
- **The Spirit of Judgment**
- **The Spirit of Burning**
- **The Spirit of Grace and of Supplications**
- **The Spirit of Wisdom and Understanding**
- **The Spirit of the Fear of the Lord**

- **The Spirit of Counsel and Might**
- **The Spirit of His Mouth**
- **The Spirit of The Father**
- **The Spirit of Truth**
- **The Spirit of Holiness**
- **The Spirit of Life**
- **The Spirit of Adoption**
- **The Spirit of Promise**
- **The Spirit of Faith**
- **The Glory Hand of God**
- **The Comforter**
- **The Power of the Highest and The Eternal**
- **The Holy Ghost**

These names are used to identify the Holy Spirit which helps us with insight into His nature and function as part of the Trinity.

Below are descriptions of a few of His names:

- ***The Spirit of the Living God*** reflects the point that God is alive and active in our midst today. *-2 Corinthians 3:3*

"Forasmuch as ye are manifestly declared to be the epistle of Christ ministered by us, written not with ink; but with the Spirit of the living God; not in tables of stone, but in fleshy Tables of the heart."

- ***The Spirit of Judgment and the Spirit of Burning*** reflects the fact that the Holy Spirit is involved in matters of justice, law, and order. The result of ***burning*** reflects that He also works in the area of purging, consuming, and purifying. The Holy Spirit cannot tolerate sin because He is ***Holy***. He is eternally committed to exposing evil and sin wherever and whenever they exist. *Isaiah 4:4*

"When the Lord shall have washed away the filth of the daughters of Zion, and shall have purged the blood of Jerusalem from the midst thereof by the spirit of judgment, and by the spirit of burning."

- ***The Spirit of Grace and of Supplications*** reveal yet another truth. Grace is unmerited favor with God. The Spirit of Grace brings us the love, mercy, and grace of Jesus Christ. When we receive something from God that we **do not** deserve (for example we received Jesus Christ), this is unmerited favor. When we do not receive something from God that we **do** deserve (like…to burn in Hell), that is His mercy. How marvelous and precious is the grace and the mercy of God. *Zechariah 12:10:*

"And I will pour upon the house of David, and upon the inhabitants of Jerusalem, the spirit of grace and of supplications"

- ***The Spirit of Truth*** reveals that there is no error in Him and that there is never any variation or conflict between the Spirit and the Word of God. *John 16:13:*

"Howbeit when he, the Spirit of Truth, is come, he will guide you into all truth: for he shall not speak of himself; but whatsoever he shall hear, that shall he speak…"

- ***The Spirit of Adoption*** reveals to us that we are adopted into the family of God through receiving Jesus Christ, His Son. *Romans 8:15:*

> ***"For ye have not received the spirit of bondage again to fear; but ye have received the Spirit of Adoption, whereby we cry, Abba, Father."***

The sin barrier is removed from us through Jesus' shed blood, which enables us to be reconciled back to God. Through the Spirit of Adoption, we become members of the family of God, joint heirs with Jesus Christ. *Romans 8:17:*

> ***"And if children, then heirs; heirs of God, and joint-heirs with Christ; if so be that we suffer with Him, that we may be also glorified together."***

- ***The Spirit of Promise*** seals the believer with a ***stamp of ownership***. *Ephesians 1:13:*

> ***"After that ye believed, ye were sealed with that Holy Spirit of Promise."***

Since we are now God's property, we no longer belong to Satan. Even if others try to convince us that we are the same sinners we were before receiving Christ, the Spirit of Promise bears witness with our spirit and we **know** that we are saved and are able to STAND on that promise.

- ***The Spirit of Faith*** is essential to the life of a Christian. *Romans 1:17:*

"The just shall live by faith".

The Spirit of Faith assures us of what truth is. This gives us boldness to confess His Word with conviction and power. We develop faith by reading and studying--by understanding and by hearing the Word of God. Our faith develops also by applying the Word of God in our lives. Without the baptism with the Holy Spirit, a person is very limited in his development and his effectiveness, because the infilling of the Holy Spirit ***builds*** faith. Faith causes ***action*** in our lives, producing ***change***.

- ***The Comforter*** is a promise Jesus made to His followers before He ascended to His Father. *John 14:16*

"And I will pray the Father,
and He shall give you another Comforter."

Jesus promised that this ***comforter*** would always be with us, to instruct us, and be of aid to us and assist us in times of need. ***The Comforter*** is always there to comfort, strengthen, encourage, and help us...even when **people** aren't. Isn't that glorious?

Notes as I Study the Word of God

What is the main subject of this book of the Bible?

____

Bible Verses of Focus

____

____

____

____

Chapter Outline:

____

____

____

____

____

____

____

____

____

____

____

____

____

____

What I've learned through this study of God's Word

How will I apply what I've learned to my life

Did I remember to pray today? ________

Date ________________

Appetizer 3

SYMBOLS OF THE HOLY SPIRIT

Although there are many symbols representing the Holy Spirit, it is very important to remember that symbols of the Holy Spirit are **NOT** the Holy Spirit. They are like trademarks that bring a company to mind. Trademarks represent the company. They are not the company.

Don't allow a *symbol* of the Holy Spirit to become a *substitute* for the real deal.

OIL - THE DOVE - LIVING WATER -WIND - FIRE -

are all symbols of the Holy Spirit. Just as the names of the Holy Spirit reveal His nature and activities, so do ***symbols*** of the Holy Spirit. The Holy Spirit does the work of God. Now, let us examine these symbols closer.

OIL

"It is like the precious ointment upon the head, that ran down upon the beard, even Aaron's beard; that went down to the skirts of his garments." Psalms 133:2:

In the Old Testament, oil was used in such abundance that it ran down the face and saturated their clothes. Likewise, today as the Holy Spirit ***immerses*** a person in His presence, there is something that flows through the heart--just as oil saturated the faces and clothes of men in the Old Testament.

James 5:14 tells us to anoint with oil and pray for the sick. In *Mark 6:13,* it says that we are to anoint the sick with oil. The use of oil as a symbol of the Holy Spirit is to teach us that the Holy Spirit has the ability to eliminate friction and abrasions from our bodies and lives. Oil is a very beautiful and appropriate symbol for the Holy Spirit because it penetrates, protects, soothes, purges, and cleanses. If burned, its energy produces light and warmth.

THE DOVE

The dove symbol represents the **gentleness** of the Holy Spirit. The Holy Spirit is either helped or hindered by our reaction to His leading. The Holy Spirit is a perfect **gentleman**. He will never force His will upon anyone. However, the Holy Spirit is also powerful and mighty. We cannot prevent the Holy Spirit from doing the will of God in this earth. We can give Him permission to use us or not, but His work will get done! The Holy Spirit is as gentle as a dove, and this is why we must learn to walk quietly and softly in the presence of the Holy Spirit. If our spirit is overactive or abrasive, we can stop the Holy Spirit from moving on us.

LIVING WATER

Jesus refers to the fullness of the Spirit in a believer like "***rivers of living water.***" *John 7:37-39:*

"In the last day, that great day of the feast, Jesus stood and cried, saying, If any man thirst, let him come unto me, and drink. He that believeth on me, as the scripture hath said, out of his belly shall flow rivers of living water. But this spake he of the Spirit…"

"For I will pour water upon him that is thirsty, and floods upon the dry ground: I will pour my spirit upon thy seed, and my blessings upon thine offspring." -Isaiah 44:3

Water is life to the human body. Our bodies are made up of 80 % water. Without it, our bodies will die. Likewise, without the spiritual water of the Holy Spirit, our spirits will also seem dead. Water refreshes, cleans, purifies, and brings life. This is one reason why Jesus uses water to represent the Holy Spirit. If we are ***dry***, then we must get the river of the Holy Spirit flowing through us. People are drawn to where refreshing rivers flow. It is more than a refreshing flow; it is ***life restoring*** to them. Without it, our spiritual lives will be dead.

WIND

"And suddenly there came a sound from heaven as of a rushing mighty wind, and it filled all the house where they were sitting." - Acts 2:2

The ***wind,*** which represents the Holy Spirit, is also gentle as it blows while it brings refreshing coolness. I have actually felt a literal breeze blowing through a building (with no air conditioner or windows opened), as the wind of the Holy Spirit was present.

"...he shall baptize you with Holy Ghost, and with FIRE." -Matthew 3:11

Fire is used to represent some of the activity and power of God. Fire, in its natural state, refines and can change certain objects from one form to another. Heat is used to soften an object so it can be hammered, molded, or pressed into shape. Fire, on the other hand, can consume an object, therefore removing it from existence. But it can also change the appearance of an object, purify it, light it, cleanse it, or warm it.

This is an excellent example of how the ***fire of the Holy Spirit*** is needed to change us.

In conclusion, the Holy Spirit reveals Jesus and the ways of God as we allow Him to move through us in mighty ways to accomplish the purposes He has here in the earth. Why would we even try to exist without Him?

Notes as I Study the Word of God

What is the main subject of this book of the Bible?

Bible Verses of Focus

Chapter Outline:

____

____

____

____

What I've learned through this study of God's Word

____

____

____

____

____

____

____

How will I apply what I've learned to my life

____

____

____

____

____

Did I remember to pray today? ________

Date __________________

Appetizer 4

TONGUES...WHY IS THIS NECESSARY?

God did not give us this opportunity to go around and say, "***I got something you don't got.***" It's not for bragging rights, nor to put other people down. If we have such a privilege to be empowered with the Holy Spirit with the evidence of speaking in "***unknown tongues,***" then we really need to know what that is all about.

First of all, there is more than one area where speaking in tongues is used with the people of God. The **gift of tongues** which is found in 1 Corinthians 14:13-14, requires ***interpretation of tongues*** to also be in operation.

"Wherefore let him that speaketh in an unknown tongue pray that he may interpret. For if I pray in an unknown tongue, my spirit prayeth, but my understanding is unfruitful."

That gift in the Bible has its purpose and I will explain that purpose later on under a different section. For now, I will be talking about speaking in tongues, which does not require interpretation, found in 1 Corinthians 14:1-10.

"Follow after charity, and desire spiritual gifts,..." "For he that speaketh in an unknown tongue speaketh not unto men, but unto God,..." -1 Corinthians 14:2

***"He that speaketh in an unknown tongue edifieth himself."* -1 Corinthians 14:4**

***"I would that ye ALL spake with tongues,"* -1 Corinthians 14:5**

***"There are, it may be, so many kinds of voices in the world, and none of them is without signification."* -1 Corinthians 14:10**

***"Wherefore tongues are for a sign, not to them that believe, but to them that believe not..."* -1 Corinthians 14:22**

First of all, the Bible uses the word **unknown**, but we actually know that there is nothing ***unknown*** to God. So what the Bible is saying is that the language is ***unknown*** only to the participant, if the Holy Spirit doesn't give them the understanding. Within this area of activation, our purpose is not to speak to man, but to speak to God. When we speak in an unknown tongue, we are speaking from the only perfect part of us--our ***born again spirit***. Satan doesn't have any idea what we are saying, but God does. We are literally praying the perfect prayer without interference from the devil or our own imperfections.

Just think about it. We are praying the ***perfect prayer,*** coming from the only ***perfect part of us***, going to ***a perfect God.*** How awesome is that?! As we can see, this form of speaking in unknown tongues is necessary for several other reasons as well.

1. It's Instantaneous
2. It's Universal
3. It's Supernatural
4. It's Given by God

We will take a look at some benefits.

- There are benefits in just "**speaking.**"

"And these signs shall follow them that believe; In my name shall they cast out devils; they shall speak with new tongues"
-Mark 16:17

- It is an "**initial sign**".

"For they heard them speak with tongues, and magnify God." -Acts 10:46

- It is needed for "**spiritual edification**".

"For he that speaketh in an unknown tongue edifieth himself" -1 Corinthians 14:4

- It reminds us of the ***Holy Spirit's "indwelling presence."***

"And I will pray the Father, and he shall give you another Comforter, that he may abide with you forever; Even the Spirit of truth; whom the world cannot receive, because it seeth him not, neither knoweth him: but ye know him; for he dwelleth with you, and shall be in you." -John 14:16-17

- It is a "**perfect line of communication.**"

"Likewise the Spirit also helpeth our infirmities (weaknesses): for we know not what we should pray for as we ought: But the Spirit itself (himself) maketh intercession for us with groanings which cannot be uttered (in a known language by you)." -Romans 8:26

Notes as I Study the Word of God

What is the main subject of this book of the Bible?

Bible Verses of Focus

Chapter Outline:

____

What I've learned through this study of God's Word

How will I apply what I've learned to my life

Did I remember to pray today? _______

Date ________________

Appetizer 5

TALENTS vs. MOTIVE GIFTS

There is a big difference between ***Talents*** and ***Motive Gifts***. Talents come in varying measures when we are physically born of a woman (those things that we naturally did from childhood).

The strength of one's motive gift comes when we are ***Born Again***. Motive gifts show us our position and others' position in the body of Christ so that we can mature and become what God wants us to be.

SOME REASONS WHY WE DON'T KNOW OUR GIFT

1. **Sin**
2. **Not involved enough in the things of God and the body of Christ**
3. **Trying to imitate others instead of seeking to find out who we are**
4. **Failure to analyze why certain Christian activities appeal to us**

We are all very familiar with and can usually recognize our ***talents.*** Therefore, I would like for us to take a closer look at our ***motive gifts.***

Each person is given at least one motive gift at the time they are ***born again***, with the faith to develop and use that gift.

"Having then gifts differing according to the grace that is given to us, whether <u>prophecy</u>, let us prophesy according to the proportion of faith; Or <u>ministry</u> (serving), let us wait on our ministering: or he that <u>teacheth</u>, on teaching; or he that <u>exhorteth</u>, on exhortation: he that <u>giveth</u>, let him do it with simplicity; he that <u>ruleth</u> (government), with diligence; he that sheweth <u>mercy</u>, with cheerfulness."
-Romans 12: 6-8

The seven gifts in Romans 12 together show the entire body of Christ. Jesus had all seven gifts. Usually we are very strong in one but may have traces of others. Sometimes we move in all of these gifts, but one is more outstanding than the others in our lives.

The gifts are:

1. **Prophecy**
2. **Serving (ministry)**
3. **Teaching (tutor)**
4. **Exhortation**
5. **Giving**
6. **Mercy**
7. **Ruling (organization/government)**

PROPHECY

The person having this gift has ***insight*** or ***intuitive sense*** about people and situations as they really are before God. A prophecy should encourage, exhort, and comfort people. The manifestations of this gift:

- Brings people to accountability so that they are restored through repentance
- Reveals inner heart motivations
- Brings inner conviction
- Brings awareness of God's presence
- Makes people fall to their knees in repentance and humility

Certain characteristics of a person with the motive gift of prophecy are:

- They need to express the message verbally
- They have the ability to discern character and motives of people
- They have the capacity to identify, define, and hate evil
- They have a willingness to experience brokenness to prompt brokenness in others
- They have a dependence on scriptural truth to validate authority
- They desire for outward evidence to demonstrate inward conviction
- They are very direct, frank, and persuasive in their speaking
- They are concerned for the reputation and the program of God
- They experience inward weeping and personal identification with sins of those they talk to
- They have an eagerness to have others point out their own blind spots so that they can help others

These are some *misuses* of this gift.

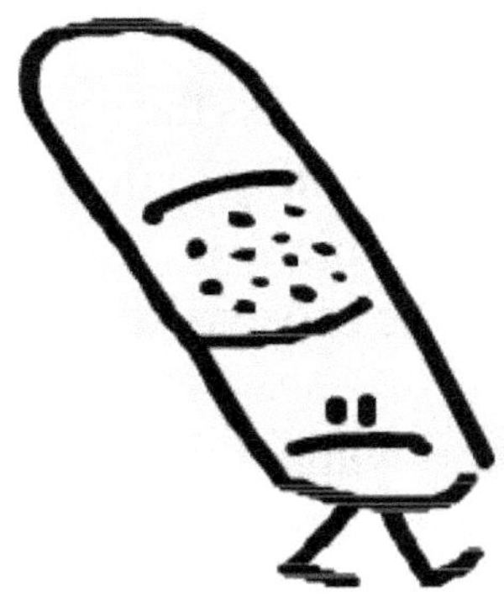

1. Correcting people who are not under our authority
2. Jumping to conclusions about words, actions, or motives
3. Having a condemning spirit, cutting off a person who has fallen
4. Dwelling on negatives
5. Demanding a smooth answer and a positive response to a harsh rebuke

Remember that ALL the gifts must be developed and that this is going to be a life-long process.

A scriptural example of a person walking with this gift is John the Baptist. He illustrates the gift of prophecy in Luke 3:3-20.

- He was aware of his unworthiness and wanted others to point out his blind spots.
- He knew he was the voice of God and depended on scriptural truth to validate his authority.
- He had directness and frankness in speaking.

- He looked for repentance in everyone with whom he spoke.
- He placed great emphasis on right and wrong and identified evil when he saw it.
- He had courage to openly reprove evil.
- He was able to discern people's motives.

TEACHING
(A Tutor of the Word, not necessarily a scholar of the Word)

A person with the motive gift of ***teaching*** teaches to impart biblical doctrine.

Certain characteristics of a person with the motive gift of teaching are:

- They have a belief that this gift is foundational to other gifts
- They places emphasis on accuracy of words (correctness)
- They test the knowledge of those who teach them
- They find delight in research for the purpose of validating truth

- They present truth in systematic sequence
- They like to avoid illustrations from non-biblical sources
- They are resistant to scriptural illustrations out of context
- They find greater joy in researching than in presenting lessons

These are some *misuses* of this gift.

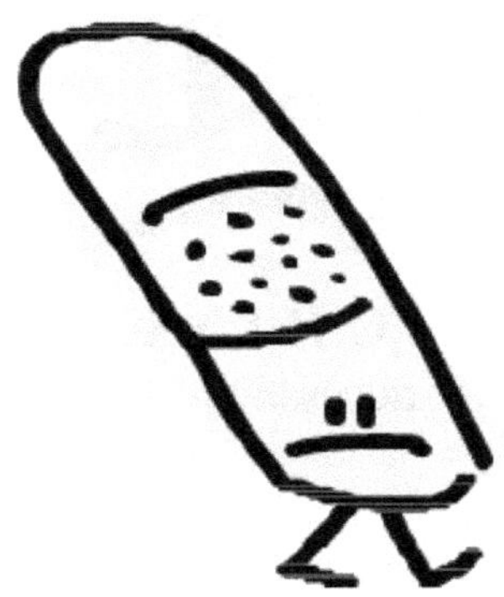

1. Becomes proud in office (or position of leadership)
2. Despises practical wisdom
3. Criticizes fine doctrine
4. Depends on human reasoning (logic)

Paul is an example of a person in scripture with the motive gift of ***teaching***.

In Luke 1-3 & 11 along with 2 Timothy 4:10-11, we recognize some of these traits.

- He felt that teaching was the most important gift
- He tested knowledge
- He tied Old and New Testaments together
- He demonstrated his endurance as he continued to research while in Arabia for 3 years and while in prison
- He did research to be able to write much of the Bible
- He did a systematic study of giving
- He had a burden to speak and impart the truth

RULING
(Organization/Government)

~ A Person who stands *in front of* ~

Certain characteristics of a person with the motive gift of ruling are:

"For this cause left I thee in Crete, that thou shouldest set in order the things that are wanting (lacking or undone), and ordain elders in every city, as I had appointed thee." -Titus 1:5

- They have the ability to see the overall picture and clarify long range goals
- They have the motivation to organize what they are responsible for
- They desire to complete tasks as quickly as possible
- They have an awareness of resources available to complete a task
- They have a tendency to stand on the sidelines until those in charge tell them to take over

- They have a tendency to assume responsibility if no structured leadership exists
- They have a willingness to endure reactions from workers in order to accomplish the ultimate goal
- They receive fulfillment in seeing others come together and enjoy a completed task
- They desire to move on to a new challenge when a previous task is completed

These are some *misuses* of this gift.

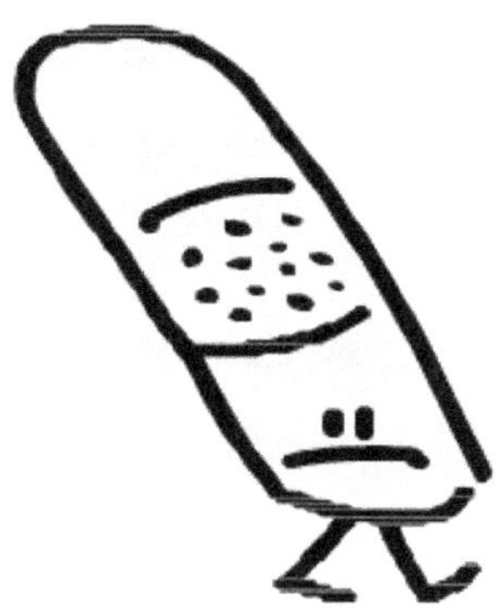

1. They see people as resources and not as people
2. They use people to accomplish personal goals
3. They are usually closed to valid complaints or suggestions
4. They sometimes fail to give proper explanation or praise

A person in scripture with this ***organizational gift*** is Nehemiah.

- He had special zeal for the cause of God's people. (Nehemiah 1:4)
- He sensed the overall problems and surveyed the needs. (Nehemiah 2:12-15)
- He knew others had to do work. (Nehemiah 2:16-18)
- He had a sense of timing. (Nehemiah 2:6)
- He organized human and material resources. (Nehemiah 3)
- He measured and proceeded under opposition. (Nehemiah 4 & 6)
- He was tough enough to face disorder from workers. (Nehemiah 5:1-13, 7:3-4, 13:11)
- He made things easy for others and was not a personal burden. (Nehemiah 5:14-19)
- He knew how to delegate authority and could sense who could best do the job. (Nehemiah 7:1-2)

GIVING

The person with the gift of ***giving*** recognizes the fact that there is a spiritual need to give and is willing to ***spend*** one's life and resources for others.

Certain characteristics of a person with the motive gift of giving are:

- They possess the ability to make wise purchases and investments
- They desire to give quietly to effective ministries and projects
- They attempt to use their giving to motivate others to give
- They are alert to valid needs they think others may overlook
- Their enjoyment in meeting needs is without pressure of appeals
- They get joy when their gift is an answer to others' prayers
- They do have a dependency on partner's counsel to confirm amount of gift
- They are concerned that their gift is of high quality
- They desire to feel a part of the work or person to whom they give

Misunderstandings concerning a *Giver*

1. Their need to deal with large sums of money may appear to be a focus on temporal values

2. Their desire to give to a ministry may appear as an attempt to control the work or the person
3. Their attempt to encourage others to give may appear as added pressure on that individual, and others could make an assumption that they lack generosity
4. Their lack of response to pressure appeals may appear as lack of generosity
5. Their frugal personal living may appear to others as selfishness in not meeting friends' or relatives' needs

New Testament Clues

- Sharing material things..........Luke 3:11
- Sharing spiritual gifts............Romans 1:11
- Sharing finances from ones own wages.......................Ephesians 4:8
- Sharing oneself..................1 Thessalonians 2:8
- Sharing the Gospel..............1 Thessalonians 2:8

Abraham is a Bible example of a ***giver***.

- He was called "friend of God" because he had a giving relationship with others (James 2:23)
- He was given assets by God. (Genesis 13:2)
- He dealt generously with others. (Genesis 13:9-10)
- He helped others when they had a need
- He wanted God to get the glory for his giving
- He would sacrifice all (Isaac) if he knew God required it
- He wanted his assets to be used for the best results
- He was concerned about the price of things and knew their value (Genesis 23)
- He rejoiced when his giving was related to answered prayers

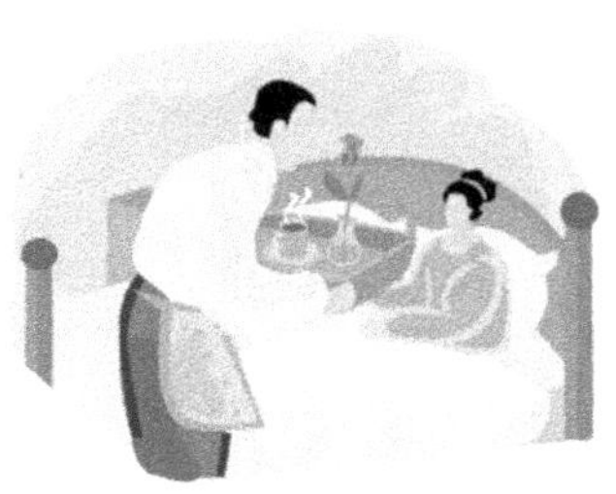

SERVING

A person with the gift of ***serving*** meets practical needs of others in love. This person demonstrates love in ***deeds,*** not only in ***words,*** by seeing what needs to be done and making himself available to get it done.

Certain characteristics of a person with the motive gift of serving are:

- Has ability to recall likes and dislikes of people
- Has alertness to detect and meet practical needs
- Meets needs as quickly as possible
- Has physical stamina without regard to weariness
- Uses personal funds to avoid delay in meeting a need
- Has sincere appreciation and can spot insincerity
- Wants to see a job done and will do extra work to accomplish it
- Involves himself in a lot of activities because of an inability to say no
- Enjoys short range goals more than long range goals
- Is frustrated with time limits on jobs

Misunderstandings concerning a *server*

1. When trying to meet needs, they may appear to be pushy
2. When hindered, they may do jobs themselves to avoid red tape
3. When eager to serve, they may be misunderstood as wanting to advance themselves
4. When working with those having different motive gifts, they may get upset with them
5. When receiving offers of help, they may find it difficult to accept them
6. When desiring appreciation, they may have feelings hurt
7. When desiring to help others, they may interfere with God's dealing with others
8. When meeting practical needs, they may be judged as lacking interest in spiritual needs
9. When enduring with stamina, they may be misinterpreted as insensitive to others' desire to serve
10. While enjoying short range goals, they may be frustrated and disorganized by long range goals
11. When directed by the pastor, they may instead get side tracked with others' needs

A Bible example of this kind of person was Martha. (Luke 10:38-41 and John 12:2)

- Martha was doing the work herself
- Martha tried to make Mary do what she was doing
- She had too many things to do because she couldn't say no
- She seemed to concentrate more on tasks than the person being served
- She saw the short range goal (cooking the meal and cleaning), rather than the long range goal (depth of Jesus)

Servers need sincere appreciation. They are workers and not ***feelers.*** They sometimes work to receive the love of others.

EXHORTATION

A person having the gift of ***exhortation*** is a very positive person who encourages people into abundant living. They love people and want the Word to become flesh in others' lives.

Certain characteristics of a person with the motive gift of exhortation are:

- Desires to visualize specific achievements and give steps of action
- Avoids systems of information that lack practical application
- Sees how tribulation can produce new levels of maturity
- Depends on individual acceptance when speaking to people
- Insights into human experience that can be applied to the Bible
- Enjoys seeing people taking steps of action to meet needs
- Grieves when teaching doesn't have practical application
- Delights in personal conferences that result in new insights

Misunderstandings concerning an *exhorter*

1. Emphasis on steps of action may seem to over simplify the problem

2. Urgency in giving steps of action may appear as having too much confidence in them
3. Desire to win non-Christians by living examples may appear as lack of interest in personal evangelism
4. Use of scripture for practical application may appear to take scripture out of context
5. Emphasis on steps of action may appear to not have awareness of others' feelings

Seven Bible examples of Exhortation

1. How one ought to live ....1 Thessalonians 4:1
2. How to please God.....................1 Thessalonians 4:1
3. How to live a life worthy of God.....1 Thessalonians 2:11
4. How to progress in love...............1 Thessalonians 4:10
5. How to live so there is
   respect among people...........1 Thessalonians 4:11 & 12
6. How to face trials.................................Acts 14:22
7. How to understand chastening.............Hebrews 12:3-5

Barnabas is an example of an exhorter in the Bible.

- Appealed to peoples' will with his message
- Was concerned with how people live (Acts 14:22)
- Was personal and practical (Acts 9:27)
- Didn't give up on Mark, but exhorted him (Acts 15:39)

MERCY

This person is happy to show ***mercy*** and has an outward manifestation of pity (always help in times of trouble).

Certain characteristics of a person with the motive gift of ***mercy*** is:

- Ability to feel atmosphere of joy or distress in an individual or in groups
- Attraction to and understanding of people in distress
- Desires to remove hurts from others' lives
- Greater concern for mental distress than physical distress
- Avoidance of being firm unless they can see how it brings benefits
- Sensitivity to words and actions that can hurt others
- Ability to discern true motives of people
- Enjoys unity with others who are sensitive to people's needs
- Closing of spirit to those who are insincere or insensitive

Misunderstandings concerning a person with the gift of *mercy*

1. Avoidance of firmness may appear to be weakness
2. Sensitivity to spirits and feelings may cause others to believe they are led by emotions and not reason
3. The desire to comfort others in distress may be misinterpreted as interest in that person
4. Constant forgiveness of a person regardless of repeated offenses may be misinterpreted as letting them run over you
5. Ability to detect insincere motives may make it difficult to know and get close to the person

The Good Samaritan is an example of the mercy gift in the Bible.

- Wanted to do something for a stranger
- Spent his resources to help and took action
- Had insight to know inn keeper would help him take care of the man
- Stimulated others to have mercy, too

Notes as I Study the Word of God

What is the main subject of this book of the Bible?

Bible Verses of Focus

Chapter Outline:

What I've learned through this study of God's Word

How will I apply what I've learned to my life

Did I remember to pray today? _______

Date _______________

Appetizer 6

SPIRITUAL GIFTS

There are ***Nine Gifts of the Spirit***, sometimes called ***Charismatic Gifts***. These nine gifts have been separated into three classifications and are found in 1 Corinthians 12.

The Word of God is very clear on the fact that all of the gifts (as different as they may be) were given by the ***same Spirit and the same Lord.***

"Now there are diversities of gifts, but the same Spirit. And there are differences of administrations, but the same Lord. And there are diversities of operations, but it is the same God which worketh all in all:"
-1 Corinthians 12:4-6

"For to one is given by the Spirit the word of wisdom; to another the word of knowledge by the same Spirit; To another faith by the same Spirit; to another the gifts of healing by the same Spirit; To another the working of miracles; to another prophecy; to another discerning of spirits; to another divers kinds of tongues; to another the interpretation of tongues."
-1 Corinthians 12:8-10

1. **Three Spoken** (vocal or inspiration gifts)
    a) Divers Kinds of Tongues (gift of tongues)
    b) Interpretation of Tongues
    c) Gift of Prophecy

2. **Three Power**
    a) Working of Miracles
    b) Gift of Faith
    c) Working of Healing

3. **Three Revelation**
    a) Word of Knowledge
    b) Word of Wisdom
    c) Discerning of Spirits

SPOKEN

1a. **<u>DIVERSE KINDS OF TONGUES</u>**:

This is not to be confused with speaking in tongues from the ***baptism with the Holy Spirit***. Private devotional tongues are for prayer, worship, and communication with God. Those do not require interpretation. However, ***diverse kinds of tongues,*** the gift of tongues, do.

This gift is given by Almighty God, to a God chosen individual, for man and therefore must be understood by man. Paul said in 1 Corinthians 14:13:

> "***Wherefore let him that speaketh in an unknown tongue pray that he may interpret.***"

He is referring to the **gift of tongues**. Praying in the ***spirit*** is not the ***gift of tongues***. When the ***gift of tongues*** is in operation, the ***gift of interpretation of tongues*** should be, too.

1b. INTERPRETATION OF TONGUES:

As stated above, this gift is in operation following the ***gift of tongues***. This gift helps create a reverence for the Lord. It is designed to guide and direct our lives and helps to reveal God to us and enhance our responses to Him. When the gift of the Spirit operates and a message is delivered in an unknown tongue, the utterance should be interpreted. The devotional tongue does not require interpretation.

1c. GIFT OF PROPHECY

This gift is usually brought to a group of believers but it may be for one or more of the individuals present at that time. Words spoken to us by the ***gift of prophecy***, should by no means guide us through life, but only confirm what God has already placed in our spirit. Even though there is evidence of many false prophets, if our spirit doesn't bear witness with a word of prophecy spoken over our life, it doesn't necessarily mean that this person is a false prophet. Sometimes, we may need to put that word aside for a period of time until other things are in place to bear witness of that which the prophecy was stating.

Today, there are a lot of false prophecies going forth by counterfeit, self-appointed prophets. They are tools used by Satan to confuse and deceive the body of Christ (the church). Do not be deceived by Satan's devices. It is his job to use every means necessary to get us side tracked from our God given mission. Don't let him.

When we are given a prophecy by a true prophet, our job is to receive it, believe it, and to position ourselves for that word to come to pass. God can lead and guide our car once it's on the road moving, but it's our job to start the engine and put it into drive. Even with a great navigational system on hand, a parked car will never get to its destination if it stays in park. Faith is an ***action*** word, and we know that faith without works is dead.

Prophecy is not primarily for giving predictions. As stated in 1 Corinthians 14:3, it is for edification, exhortation, and comfort. If someone prophesies doom, damnation, and judgment on an individual or a group, it is not from God or God's Holy Spirit--who is a gentleman. Paul wrote:

"Despise not prophesying. Prove all things; hold fast that which is good." -1 Thessalonians 5:20-21

Prophecy should always be judged. There has been misuse of this gift many times, but that should not deter our faith in the true and proper use of God's gifts.

2a. **WORKING OF MIRACLES**

POWER

The miracle of conversion (when one receives salvation) is perhaps the greatest miracle in the world today, but the miracle of salvation is not what is meant by the ***working of miracles***. Miracles are incidents or events that occur which seem to defy ***the natural laws*** of the earth. Jesus, as we are well aware, performed more miracles than anyone else in the Bible. Even so, He said,

"Greater works than these shall you do; because I go unto My Father."
-John 14:12

God delights in performing miracles today and using His people to deliver this gift. All God given miracles will bring glory to Him, not us. Remember, Satan can perform miracles also, but he will never give the glory to God.

If we have been blessed with this gift, it can be very exciting, but the miracles are never meant to take our attention away from Jesus. We don't follow miracles...follow Jesus and the miracles will follow us.

Jonah and the Whale (Jonah 1:17)

Moses and the parting of the Red Sea

Miracles performed ***through*** man ***by*** God. (Exodus 15:8)

2b. GIFT OF FAITH

Faith is believing ***before*** seeing the accomplishments of a situation. Faith eventually brings into reality what a person starts out believing. Faith is not passive, but active.

The ***gift of faith***, on the other hand, is different from faith spoken about above. It is not even like the ***faith*** we receive as a ***fruit of the spirit***, which will be explained in more detail later on in our studies. The fruit of the spirit's ***faith*** takes time to develop. The ***gift of faith*** is not the ***measure of faith*** spoken of in Romans 12:3. The ***gift of faith*** is given by God instantaneously with no delay. With this gift, there is a ***sudden surge*** of ***special faith*** that usually occurs in a crisis situation and within the pressure of a great need.

Remember that all of these nine gifts are given ***as the Holy Spirit wills***, not as we will. It's totally up to Holy Spirit's timing, even though the Bible tells us to desire spiritual gifts. We are thankful for Him doing things as He wills, and for doing them His way.

2c. GIFT OF HEALING

The gifts of healing are for supernatural cures. The Holy Spirit works through yielded human vessels to channel

God's healing power to those in need. Again, it is as the ***Holy Spirit wills.*** If it were up to us, we would be in every hospital in every nation and we would probably be taking ***all the credit***. It is not up to us to question God's motive for not allowing the Holy Spirit to manifest healing more often. We must remain thankful for Him being willing to do it at all, when He is ready.

When the ***gift of healing*** is in operation, people are instantly healed; saved people and unsaved people alike. It is not a gift that we can turn on and off as we chooses to, or the hospitals would be empty today.

Usually, when the ***gift of healing*** is in operation, the ***gift of miracles*** and the ***gift of faith*** are also in operation at the same time. We can see why. It is amazing what God can do through a yielded vessel.

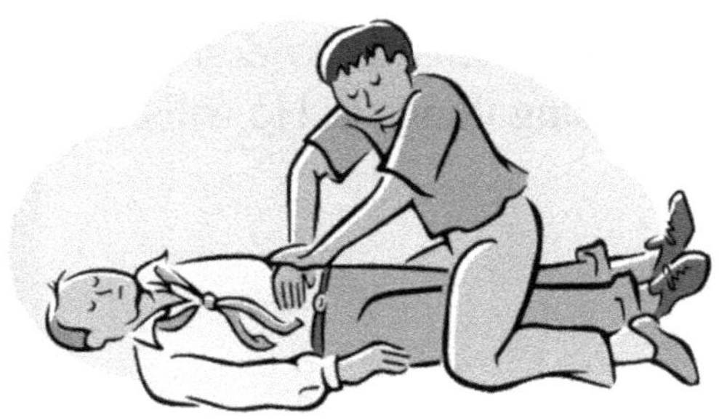

R E V E L A T I O N

3a. **WORD OF KNOWLEDGE**

A ***word of knowledge*** is not what we ***know***, but pertains to what we ***don't know***. It doesn't matter how intelligent or unintelligent we are, our educational background or level of experience don't hold anything to a ***word of knowledge.*** The word of knowledge is a supernatural revelation from God through a chosen individual. It is the very ***mind of God*** concerning people, places, things, or events. It can pertain to things of the past or the present.

3b. **WORD OF WISDOM**

This is different from the wisdom discussed in James 1:5.

"If any of you lack wisdom, let him ask of God, that giveth to all men liberally, and upbraideth not; and it shall be given him."

This is referring to normal wisdom. The wisdom that we need for our daily operations is normal wisdom. The ***gift of wisdom*** is not referring to simply being wise, clever, or quick witted, but rather the ***mind of God*** pertaining to ***futuristic*** events. Only God has the knowledge of what is to come. The virgin birth was given by the ***word of wisdom*** found in Isaiah 7:14.

"Therefore the Lord himself shall give you a sign; Behold, a virgin shall conceive, and bear a son"...

The ***word of wisdom*** is still very much in operation TODAY. Will the Holy Spirit work through us in this area?

3c. DISCERNING OF SPIRITS

The gift of the ***word of knowledge*** and the gift of the ***discerning of spirits*** generally work together, however if needed, can work independently. There are different levels of discernment. Believers and non-believers both possess natural discernment. It's simply a matter of using what is known as ***common sense*** to evaluate people, circumstances, activities, and situations. Then we have a deeper discernment available to those who have the ***mind of Christ*** by being ***born again***. Still, this must be developed as a Christian grows in Jesus while they apply what they have learned.

> ***"For everyone that useth milk is unskillful in the word of righteousness: for he is a babe. But strong meat belongeth to them that are of full age, even those who by reason of use has their senses exercised to discern both good and evil."***
> ***-Hebrews 5:13-14***

Do you see how important it is, to activate, with wisdom, the things you learn in God's Word. Who wants to remain a babe?

This gift manifests itself at the very moment it is needed. The yielded believer is immediately able to sense the motivating force behind an individual or see under the surface of a particular situation. The believer may at that moment be able to, actually see demonic spirits and/or angelic beings at work. This gift is extremely beneficial and necessary during this day and age. It can function as a form of protection as more satanic attacks than ever are being sent forth against Christians today.

Demonic forces are always at work and must be dealt with. The gift of discerning of spirits is needed today and is available for our use, but remember that all of these gifts belong to the Holy Spirit. He will allow them to operate through you only as He wills. We Christians are to ***desire*** spiritual gifts. . .

So Go For It, Saints!

Notes as I Study the Word of God

What is the main subject of this book of the Bible?

____

Bible Verses of Focus

____

____

____

____

Chapter Outline:

____

____

____

____

____

____

____

____

____

____

____

____

____

____

What I've learned through this study of God's Word

How will I apply what I've learned to my life

Did I remember to pray today? ______

Date ______________

Appetizer 7
THE FRUIT OF THE SPIRIT

As we develop the ***fruit of the spirit*** in our lives, others will see ***Jesus*** in us and be attracted to ***Him***, not ***us***. It is in the midst of very trying times, such as those today, that God may work through us to touch others' lives for Jesus.

One of the main functions of the third person of the Godhead, the Holy Spirit, is to impart God's holiness to us. He accomplishes this as He develops within us a Christ-like character, which is marked by the ***fruit of the spirit***. God has a purpose for this. He wants us to become ***mature*** and attain the full measure of perfection that is found in Jesus Christ.

"Till we all come in the unity of the faith, and of the knowledge of the Son of God, unto a perfect man, unto the measure of the stature of the fullness of Christ."
-Ephesians 4:13

Unlike the ***gifts of the spirit***, the ***fruit of the spirit*** is not divided among believers. ***Joy*** is not given to one and ***peace*** given to another. Instead ***all*** Christians should be marked by ***all*** the ***fruit of the spirit.*** It is just a matter of developing different parts of our character until it displays what God intended it to display (which is Him in us).

Have you ever wondered why the Bible talks about the ***fruit*** of the spirit rather than ***fruits***? An apple tree that we pull an apple from bears many apples, but they all come from the same tree. Likewise, the Holy Spirit is the source of all ***fruit*** in our lives.

It is more than our normal character; it is our born again character we are referring to. No, it's not all together as it should be the very moment we receive Jesus into our life, but this is the starting point where God can begin His work in us. The fruit of the spirit is placed down in our born again spirit and all the fruit of the spirit must be developed.

"But the fruit of the Spirit is love, joy, peace, longsuffering, gentleness, goodness, faith, meekness, temperance: against such there is no law." -Galatians 5:22-23

We see a lot of fences around people's homes with gates for entering and exiting. Well, a gate can be used for two purposes:

1. It can be opened to let people in.
2. It can be shut to keep people out.

Well, let us look at those gates, spiritually. Spiritually, those gates are like our lives. We have all sorts of junk in our lives. Of course, this junk does not please God and frankly, He wants it out of our lives. We must allow the Holy Spirit to come in and take control of the mess. Unfortunately, without the Holy Spirit, we cannot even open the gate. So, when we allow the Holy Spirit to open the gate of our hearts, we yield to Him and allow our fruit to develop our character in all areas, but maybe in one area at a time.

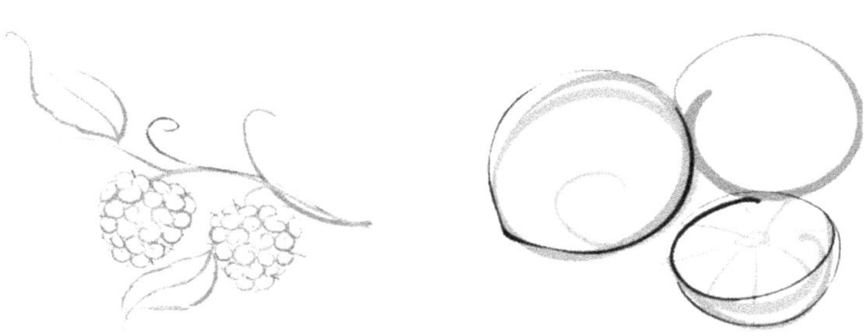

The Bible says that the Holy Spirit wants us to have fruit, and then more fruit, and even much fruit. Scripture also tells us that we can only bear spiritual fruit if we ***abide in Christ***. Scripture tells us that apart from the Lord, we can do nothing.

However, it is possible to make use of the ***gifts of the Spirit*** even when we are out of fellowship with God, because those gifts are without repentance. Remember, those gifts operate as ***the Holy Spirit wills.*** But, we can in no way display the ***fruit of the spirit*** with an ugly disposition. Even unrepented sin in our lives will disrupt our relationship with God and His characteristics won't manifest through us.

LOVE

"By this all men will know that you are my disciples, if you have LOVE for one another." -John 13:35

The greatest mark of the Christian is certainly LOVE. No matter how many ways we may walk out our testimonies, the absence of love will void them all.

"...and if I deliver my body to be burned, but do not have Love, it profits me nothing." -1 Corinthians 13:3

JOY

The joy which the ***Spirit*** brings to our lives lifts us above situations and circumstances of any magnitude. When

Jesus met with His disciples in the Upper Room, He told them that He had spoken as He did...

"that my JOY may be in you, and that your JOY may be made full." -John 15:11

Have you taken a look at our world today? How about our schools or even some churches? Our world seems ***joyless***, full of disillusionment and fear. Even many of the superficial joys and pleasures of life are also disappearing. However, we who have been born again should not be alarmed. Remember that old song that says:

This joy that I have
The world didn't give it to me
The world didn't give it....The world can't take it away.

There is a lot of truth in this song. As a matter of fact, it's very true to scripture. The Bible teaches us that our spiritual joy is not dependent on circumstances. The Holy Spirit directs His joy to our deepest problems and hurts, if we allow Him to. This makes it possible for us to be filled with JOY in the midst of any and every circumstance.

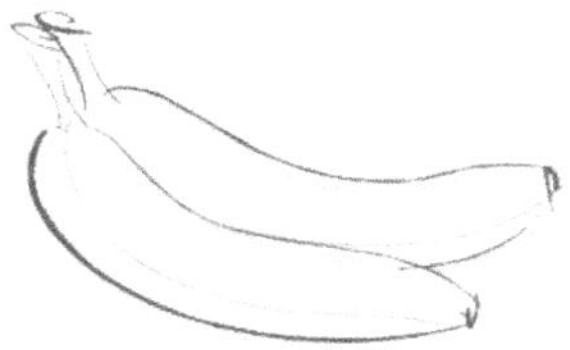

Think about God's joy radiating through you, not your own pumped up joy. Do you know how much joy God sees when He thinks about who you are in Him? Who you will become? Operate from His point of reference and get your joy back.

PEACE

There are a lot of different attributes when we think about ***peace.*** It carries with it unity, rest, ease, completeness, and security. God reveals Himself to us in the Old Testament as ***Jehovah Shalom,*** our peace. Isaiah said,

> ***"Thou wilt keep him in perfect peace, whose mind is stayed on Thee." -Isaiah 26:3***

When we give in to worry, we deny the Holy Spirit the right to lead us into confidence and peace. Do we really know who holds our future in His hands? Don't tremble on a rock, because we know who made the rock. We shouldn't doubt because we know the ONE who erases all doubt. Do we have peace today? It is only a decision away.

PATIENCE

This part of the ***fruit of the spirit*** is demonstrated in our relationships with our neighbors. This fruit is thought of as patiently enduring ill-treatment without anger or seeking revenge. ***Patience*** from the fruit of the spirit, judges the faults of others without unjust criticism. Patience also includes perseverance. This is the ability to stand up under weariness, strain, and persecution while doing the work of the Lord. Paul teaches us that we can be...

"Strengthened with all might, according to His glorious power, unto all patience and longsuffering with joyfulness."
-Colossians 1:11

"Weeping may last for the night, but a shout of joy comes in the morning."
-Psalms 30:5

GENTLENESS
(Kindness)

Gentleness washes away all that is harsh. Some Christians seem to have such a passion for righteousness that they have no room left for compassion for those who have fallen.

Jesus was ***gentle and kind*** to those who had failed or fallen short. The only people Jesus dealt harshly with were the hypocritical religious leaders, and we should take that same approach.

"The servant of the Lord must not strive;
but be GENTLE unto all men."
-2 Timothy 2:24

Gentleness is not a sign of weakness, as many may think. A gentle heart is a broken heart--a heart that weeps over the sins of the wicked as well as the sacrifices of the saved.

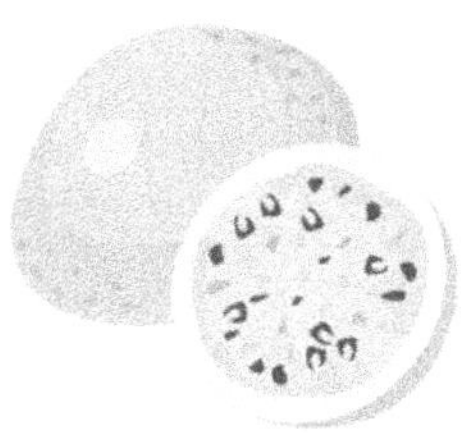

GOODNESS

Goodness is love in action. It is doing good out of a willing heart to please God, not ourselves or man. We expect no medals or thank-you notes, nor rewards in return. Christ wants this kind of ***goodness*** to be demonstrated by every Christian, but it will take a process of development and a lot of practice to accomplish it. It may take a life time, but don't get discouraged. Just take one situation after another and apply goodness as we believe God would.

FAITHFULNESS

Faithfulness is ***loyalty or devotion called to duty*** produced by the Holy Spirit in a yielded Christian's life. Loyalty in the little things is one of the surest tests of character an individual can demonstrate.

"...thou hast been faithful over a few things, I will make Thee ruler over many things."
-Matthew 25:21

God has given us certain responsibilities as mature Christians. When we refuse to accept these responsibilities, we are unfaithful. As we yield by saying ***yes*** to God's will, the Holy Spirit will begin to perform the deeper work of God's plan in our lives.

One day, all Christians will stand before Jesus to give an account of the works we have done since we received Him. We will be judged, not on the basis of how successful we were in the eyes of people, but on how faithful we were in the areas to which God has called us.

MEEKNESS

We have a misconception with the word ***meekness***. Nowhere in the Bible does this word mean ***spiritless or timid***. The ***meekness*** here carries the idea of being tame, like a wild horse that has been broken. In the Bible, Peter is an example of a person who had a rough character until he allowed the Holy Spirit to tame him.

Meekness is actually power, strength, spirit, and wildness under control. This kind of inward, quiet strength as a work of the Holy Spirit does not come on a playground, but on a spiritual battleground. A lot of intercession must take place to tame our will, and we must be willing to submit. Remember, the Holy Spirit is a gentleman and will not force us to do anything. So go for it, saints, because one day "***the meek will inherit the earth.***"
-Matthew 5:5

SELF CONTROL
(temperance)

This fruit helps us to control our actions and thoughts.

"***Those who live according to their sinful nature have their minds set on what that nature desires; but those who live in accordance with the Spirit have their minds set on what the Spirit desires.***"
-Romans 8:5 NIV

- Temperance in relation to sin is abstinence
- Temperance in matters of dress is appropriate modesty
- Temperance in our consumption of food is moderation
- Temperance in sexual matters is abstinence for the unmarried
- Temperance with respect to alcohol is sobriety

- Temperance in regard to temper is self control
- Temperance in defeat is hopefulness

In Proverbs it states that "a man without self-control is as defenseless as a city with broken down walls." If we, as Christians, fail to allow the Holy Spirit to develop the ***fruit of the spirit*** in our lives, what hope is there for the rest of the world? God has placed the ability in us to develop all the fruit. He only requires us to allow it and desire it to be developed in us.

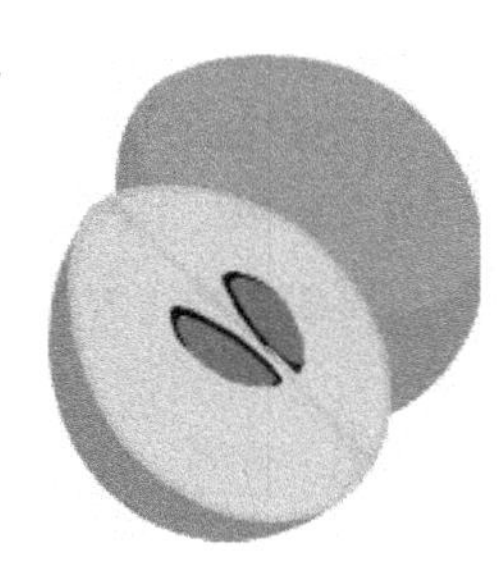

Will You Decide to Develop Godly Fruit In Your Life?

Notes as I Study the Word of God

What is the main subject of this book of the Bible?

Bible Verses of Focus

Chapter Outline:

____

____

____

____

What I've learned through this study of God's Word

____

____

____

____

____

____

____

How will I apply what I've learned to my life

____

____

____

____

____

Did I remember to pray today? ________

Date __________________

Appetizer 8

MINISTRY GIFTS

"And He gave some, apostles; and some, prophets; and some, evangelists; and some, pastors, and teachers."
-Ephesians 4:11

God gave us these gifts when He ascended on high, taking with Him the Old Testament saints who had died their physical death and were waiting in Paradise--Abraham's bosom.

"Wherefore he saith, when he ascended up on high, he led captivity captive, and gave gifts unto men. Now that he ascended, what is it but that he also descended first into the lower parts of the earth?
-Ephesians 4:8-9

Well, you might ask, "***Why did Jesus give these gifts to man?***" I'm so glad you asked.

"For the perfecting of the saints, for the work of the ministry, for the edifying of the body of Christ."
-Ephesians 4:12

1. For the perfecting of the saints.

The body of Christ will never reach perfection without ALL of these gifts operating in His church. Know, too, that this is a ***process.***

2. For the work of the ministry.

The work of the ministry is not easy. There must be supernatural intervention to accomplish all that God has intended for us to accomplish here on this earth. He would never expect us to do this without giving us the proper tools to get His work done. We must recognize those tools, embrace them, develop them, and USE them.

3. For the edifying of the Body of Christ.

Edifying means to ***build up.*** Don't you think the saints of God need to be built up continuously in order to stay consistent in the work of the ministry? Sure we do. God's plans to help equip us for the ministry were set in place before the foundations of the world. We must trust His plans and His processes for our lives.

How long do you think those ***ministry gifts*** are suppose to be around? Well, let's go to the His Word and see.

"Till we all come in the unity of the faith, and of the knowledge of the Son of God, unto a perfect man, unto the measure of the stature of the fullness of Christ." -Ephesians 4:13

- Until we all come in the unity of the faith. Are we all there yet?
- Until we all know everything we need to know about the Son of God.
- Until we are perfect men. Need I say more?
- Until we know the measure of the stature of the fullness of Christ. Wow!

So, from examining this passage of scripture, we should have those gifts operating in the Church until Jesus comes.

Please know that ***man*** cannot ***call*** us into this area of ministry. God does the ***calling***. He calls us and He identifies the specific area of that call. We don't enter this area of ministry because there is a ***need*** in the church. We must be absolutely certain that God has called us, or we will be eaten alive. However, if God has truly called us, He knows what He is doing, and no one and nothing can take us out!

I'm not implying that we are already perfect. Remember that we will always be a ***work in progress,*** but God can complete what He has begun in us, if we trust, believe, and seek His training. Know that we will need ***a lot of training***, no matter how smart we think we already are. On the other hand, God will train us (if we want Him to), no matter how unequipped or unworthy we think we are. No one is "worthy" of a call like this on their lives. It's only by God's grace and favor that He has chosen us in the first place.

We can't take any credit for that… so don't try. On the other hand, don't get wrapped up in "false humility" either. We need to be confident in the awesome task that God has called us to do, and the awesome abilities He's placed in us to get that job done. We are fearfully and wonderfully made. We should not be ashamed of what He has placed in us. We must keep a balance about our calling.

Let's look closer at these five ***Ministry Gifts*** in more detail.

The first ministry gift of the Church is that of the ***Apostle***. An Apostle has been called to set proper order in the house of God, but also to help establish other ministries. They will assist other churches with guidelines and foundational structure so that they will be able to stand under pressure. They flow in their gift. Here are some characteristics of people called to this area of ministry:

- They are full of wisdom and have keen insight to discern the motives of others.
- They operate according to order and protocol and teach others to do the same.
- They have a serious passion for the nations and lands of the earth.
- They have a heart for training leaders and are good at it. Other leaders are naturally drawn to them.
- They possess a wealth of problem solving skills and excellent management skills.
- They are disciplined in handling their personal affairs.

The next ministry gift is that of the ***Prophet***. A prophet is called to speak forth divine messages or revelations directly from the mouth of God. Some characteristics of a Prophet are:

- They are skilled at being led by the Holy Spirit to wage war on the enemy and to bring about deliverance of others by speaking a ***spirit led word*** over them.
- They are natural intercessors and have a keen sensitivity to the voice of God.
- They have supernatural gifts of discernment and interpretation of tongues.
- They are persons of integrity in their personal affairs.
- They seek God's face for His voice and His heart.
- They are very sensitive to being accurate in their delivery of God's message to others.
- They are usually perceived by others as being too vocal, too serious, and too impatient.

Another ministry gift is that of the ***Evangelist.*** An Evangelist's heart is focused on the lost. Their mission is one that will convict people of their sins and let them know that there is hope in Jesus. Some characteristics of an Evangelist are:

- They have a heart to get outside of the church building and go into the streets for mission. They will not be content staying inside of a building.
- They may have an unusual burden to travel all over the world.
- They are naturally anointed to bring people to repentance.
- They can be very radical and creative in their approach to winning souls.
- They have a heart for the poor and the hurting.

The last two ministry gifts are the ***Pastor*** and the ***Teacher.*** Some preachers don't have a *natural* anointing to teach. This does not mean that they *can't* teach. A preacher's anointing is like no other, and there is a place for this ministry gift or God would not have called specific people to this area. Many lost souls only have an ear to hear great preaching. However, a person that has the ***ministry gift of a teacher,*** has a natural ability to impart understanding to others in a supernatural, simplistic manner. Both Pastors and Teachers have very similar characteristics, which are listed below:

- They both have a servant's and a shepherd's heart.
- They love people and are compassionate toward them.
- They have the ability to discern people's needs and possess supernatural wisdom.

- They are a stickler for details, and order is a must (especially for the teacher).
- They are anointed with a magnetic personality; others are drawn to them.

All of the ministry gifts are needed for the perfecting of the saints, not just two or three of them. Try operating without one or more of your fingers and see how difficult life would be. The same thing applies to the five ministry gifts. Life would be extremely difficult without any one of them. So, we must get into our proper place and develop our gift(s) to be used for His glory, and for the perfecting of the people whom God loves.

Notes as I Study the Word of God

What is the main subject of this book of the Bible?

____

Bible Verses of Focus

Chapter Outline:

What I've learned through this study of God's Word

How will I apply what I've learned to my life

Did I remember to pray today? ______

Date ______________

Appendix

Other ***Appetizers*** you will find in Volumes 1, & 3

Volume 1: You Must Be Born Again
Who Says God is 3 in 1?
3 In 1 me
Changing Your Attitude
Improving Your Thoughts
No Pain, No Gain: Costs and Benefits
When or If I Fall…Forgiveness

Volume 3: Why Prayer?
Different Types of Prayer
What Does Fasting Have to Do With Anything?
Holy Communion
Being A Good Steward
Saying No to Self-Indulgence
To Borrow or Not to Borrow
Looking at Hoarding vs. Savings
The Tithe and Various Ways of Sharing
Music, Praise & Worship

PRAYER FOR SALVATION

Dear Lord Jesus. I believe that You are the Christ, born of the virgin Mary. I believe that You died for my sins and were raised from the dead for my victories. I repent of my sins. I'm sorry, Lord. I turn away from those things that do not please You. Please come into my heart and make me Your child. Cleanse me and help me to live for You. I thank You for receiving me and by faith in your written Word, I receive Your free gift, now. In Jesus' name, Amen.

______________________________________Signature

___________________________Date

ABOUT THE AUTHOR

Minister Linda is a unique ministry gift to the body of Christ. She is an extension of the Five-Fold Ministry gift in the area of teaching with dance interpretation of the Gospel of Jesus Christ. Her experiences include the establishment of *Spirit of Praise Liturgical Outreach, Inc.*, a non-profit 501 (c) 3 organization, which not only helped to establish and oversee new dance ministries, but also extended into the communities and hospitals with a three-fold mission goal.

In addition to the books entitled, *Appetizers from the Word of God...Are You Hungry? Volume 1, 2, & 3,* Minister Linda has authored an interactive workbook and DVD entitled, *Moving from Glory to Glory through Movement*. This interactive workbook/DVD was designed to assist dance ministries in their growth and understanding using their gift of the Arts in ministry for our Lord. The accompanying DVD is a three hour workshop that includes six instructional dances taught step by step, featuring a new dance tool; veils, for the praise dancer to worship our Lord.

The *Spirit of Truth Storybooks* is the latest project Linda is developing, highlighting individual children stories from A through Z. These stories feature characters from Anxious Arlene through Zealous Zeporah, with various multicultural characters in-between. The children's series was designed to touch the hearts of children dealing with the issues of life from a child's perspective. A secret coded message has been hidden throughout the pages of each story and when decoded spells out a message of encouragement for the reader. This unique storybook is being completed in English and Spanish and will be available in 2014.

Minister Linda is a native of Suffolk, VA. She is the wife of George B. Mason, Jr. and the mother of Tamara and George III. She is a Christian and a teacher of the Gospel of Jesus Christ. Minister Linda faithfully served for seven years as Caleb's Crew Youth Ministry coordinator at Emmanuel Restoration Church (ERC) of Midlothian, Virginia, under the leadership of Pastors Glenn and Nona Mason. She also ministered through dance with ***Chosen Dance Ministry of ERC*** for 3 years, from its conception, which continued at her next church home; Hosanna Victory Church. Minister Linda has an Associate Degree in Early Childhood Education and a background in insurance. She is now an Independent Business Owner with a passion for writing and a desire to serve in ministry full time. Her goal is to have such an intimate relationship with Christ, that she becomes a walking, living example of 3 John 1:2: ***"It is my will that you prosper, be in health, even as your soul prospers."*** Her confession is: *"I shall become the balanced truth of 3 John 1:2, so that when people see me and my life, they will glorify God in Heaven and without question, cry out—*

WHAT MUST I DO TO BE SAVED?

Minister Linda C. Mason is available for:

~ Speaking Engagements ~
~Workshops & Conferences ~
~ Book Signings ~

To request Minister Mason for your church,
community or organizational function,
for prayer or consultation, please contact her:

E-Mail:

lcmason@deepseapublishing.com

For book signing events and more information about Minister Mason, please check out her author's page: www.deepseapublishing.com.

Thank you for your interest.

www.ingramcontent.com/pod-product-compliance
Lightning Source LLC
Chambersburg PA
CBHW071620040426
42452CB00009B/1412

9781939535283